MW00445289

100 QUESTIONS FOR MOM

A JOURNAL TO INSPIRE REFLECTION AND CONNECTION

AMY CARNEY

R

ROCKRIDGE
PRESS

Copyright © 2021 by Rockridge Press, Emeryville, California

No part of this publication may be reproduced, stored in a retrieval system, or transmitted in any form or by any means, electronic, mechanical, photocopying, recording, scanning, or otherwise, except as permitted under Sections 107 or 108 of the 1976 United States Copyright Act, without the prior written permission of the Publisher. Requests to the Publisher for permission should be addressed to the Permissions Department, Rockridge Press, 6005 Shellmound Street, Suite 175, Emeryville, CA 94608.

Limit of Liability/Disclaimer of Warranty: The Publisher and the author make no representations or warranties with respect to the accuracy or completeness of the contents of this work and specifically disclaim all warranties, including without limitation warranties of fitness for a particular purpose. No warranty may be created or extended by sales or promotional materials. The advice and strategies contained herein may not be suitable for every situation. This work is sold with the understanding that the Publisher is not engaged in rendering medical, legal, or other professional advice or services. If professional assistance is required, the services of a competent professional person should be sought. Neither the Publisher nor the author shall be liable for damages arising herefrom. The fact that an individual, organization, or website is referred to in this work as a citation and/or potential source of further information does not mean that the author or the Publisher endorses the information the individual, organization, or website may provide or recommendations they/it may make. Further, readers should be aware that websites listed in this work may have changed or disappeared between when this work was written and when it is read.

For general information on our other products and services or to obtain technical support, please contact our Customer Care Department within the United States at (866) 744-2665, or outside the United States at (510) 253-0500.

Rockridge Press publishes its books in a variety of electronic and print formats. Some content that appears in print may not be available in electronic books, and vice versa.

TRADEMARKS: Rockridge Press and the Rockridge Press logo are trademarks or registered trademarks of Callisto Media Inc. and/or its affiliates, in the United States and other countries, and may not be used without written permission. All other trademarks are the property of their respective owners. Rockridge Press is not associated with any product or vendor mentioned in this book.

Interior and Cover Designer: Angela Navarra
Art Producer: Sue Bischofberger
Editors: Shannon Criss and Carolyn Abate
Production Editor: Emily Sheehan
Illustration © Enliven Designs/Creative Market; Artist's Archive/Creative Market; and Digital Curio/Creative Market.
Author photo courtesy of Diana Elizabeth.
Hardcover ISBN: 978-1-63878-854-6
Paperback ISBN: 978-1-64876-400-4
R0

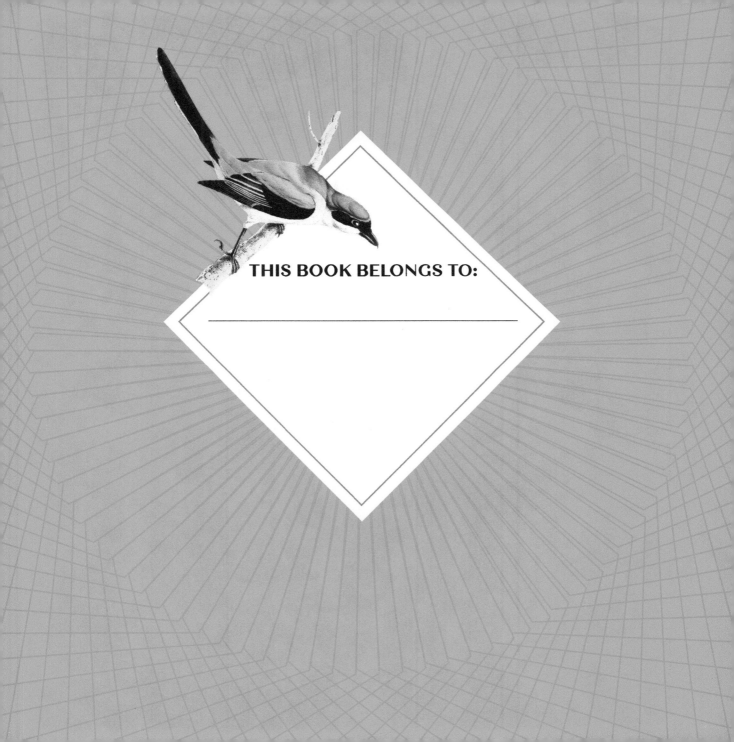

THIS BOOK BELONGS TO:

_____

CONTENTS

INTRODUCTION

Several years ago, I received an unexpected cancer diagnosis after a routine examination. During this unsettling period, I contemplated what I would want to hand down to my children if this disease were to take my life. I would want my children to know who I was before they entered my world, who I've become while raising them, and who I hope to be at the end of my life.

Fortunately, I returned to full health and with a deeper appreciation for the importance of leaving my legacy while I'm alive and able.

I have created this journal as a way for mothers to record with intention the many moments that have shaped our lives and legacies. After all, our wisdom can only be treasured by future generations if we take the time to share our stories. I welcome you to join me in this significant endeavor of putting your precious memories to paper.

To get the most out of this journal, keep in mind that there are no right or wrong ways to respond to each question. Be candid and thoughtful with your answers so your unique perspective on life and motherhood creates a treasured memoir. A great way to get started is to block off some time on your calendar, grab your favorite pen, and prepare to turn this journal into the priceless keepsake it is intended to be. Within these pages you will be prompted to recall your past and to reflect on your future. I hope that the questions–some light and fun, others deep and thought-provoking– will guide you to strengthened relationships and connections with your loved ones.

This journal also serves to help your children and future generations gain a fuller understanding of your family's origins. Your family will cherish your authentic voice coming through your handwriting on the pages, so it's important to document everything in your own words. Try not to overthink or hold back when answering the questions; instead, write freely and honestly, recording whatever comes to your mind or heart.

Take your time when completing each entry, and if you come across a question you need to ponder over longer, feel free to skip it and come back to it later. Go easy on yourself and enjoy the process. While today's technology can easily connect us to our loved ones, it can never replace the handwritten word's sustaining power in a tangible journal. And capturing the stories and memories from your life within the pages of this book ensures that your children and future generations will enjoy this keepsake for years to come.

Your motherly wisdom remains invaluable. I wish you a lifetime of beautiful moments.

PART I

THE
EARLY YEARS

So much of who we are today is defined by the experiences we have growing up in our families, homes, and communities. The early years of our lives often define our future paths.

In this section, the questions prompt you to document the details of your birth as well as speak to your family dynamic. The questions then progress to your childhood and adolescent experiences with the intention of helping your loved ones get a feel of what life was like for you growing up in your family of origin.

Through your answers, future generations will be able to better understand how growing up in your family shaped who you are today.

ORIGINS

What is your full name? Does your name hold a significant
meaning for you or your family?

_____

_____

_____

_____

_____

_____

_____

_____

_____

When were you born? Are there any **details** of your birth story you can add?

_____

_____

_____

_____

_____

_____

_____

_____

_____

_____

_____

Where were you born? List other members of your family who were also born there.

_____

_____

_____

_____

_____

_____

_____

_____

_____

What are your parents' full names? Do either of your parents have a first or middle name that's been passed down through generations?

_____

_____

_____

_____

_____

_____

_____

_____

_____

_____

Did you feel connected to both of your parents growing up, or one more than the other? Why or why not?

_____

_____

_____

_____

_____

_____

_____

_____

_____

_____

Making the decision to have a child— it's **MOMENTOUS.** It is to decide forever to **HAVE YOUR HEART** go walking around outside **YOUR BODY.**

ELIZABETH STONE

FAMILY

Do you have any siblings? If so, where are you in the birth order? If not, what was the best part of growing up as an only child?

_____

_____

_____

_____

_____

_____

_____

_____

_____

Which family member were you closest to growing up?
What made your bond strong?

_____

_____

_____

_____

_____

_____

_____

_____

_____

_____

How did your family most enjoy spending time together?

_____

_____

_____

_____

_____

_____

_____

_____

_____

_____

In what ways was your family different from other families? Why?

_____

_____

_____

_____

_____

_____

_____

_____

_____

_____

Describe your childhood home(s).

_____

_____

_____

_____

_____

_____

_____

_____

_____

_____

_____

" Call it a **CLAN,**
call it a **NETWORK,**
call it a **TRIBE,**
call it a **FAMILY.**
Whatever you call it,
whoever you are,
YOU NEED ONE.
"

JANE HOWARD

TRADITIONS

Did you travel with your family? If so, where did you go?

_____

_____

_____

_____

_____

_____

_____

_____

_____

_____

Did your family celebrate holidays during your childhood. If not, why? If they did, which one was your favorite, and why was it special to you?

_____

_____

_____

_____

_____

_____

_____

_____

_____

How did you celebrate birthdays in your family?

Which of your birthdays was the most memorable and why?

_____

_____

_____

_____

_____

_____

_____

_____

_____

Did your family eat meals together? Who did most of the cooking in your home?

_____

_____

_____

_____

_____

_____

_____

_____

_____

Name a family tradition you have carried forward into your life today.

_____

_____

_____

_____

_____

_____

_____

_____

_____

_____

_____

There is something
about saying,

'WE ALWAYS DO THIS,'

which helps keep
the years together.

EDITH SCHAEFFER

SCHOOLING

Was education valued in your family? If so, in what ways was education promoted? If not, what was valued instead?

What types of schools did you attend (i.e., private, public, faith-based, homeschool)? What did you like and dislike about where and how you were educated?

Who was your favorite teacher or instructor?
Describe why you favored them.

_____

_____

_____

_____

_____

_____

_____

_____

_____

_____

What subjects did you enjoy learning?
Which could you have done without?

_____

_____

_____

_____

_____

_____

_____

_____

_____

_____

Did you attend college? If so, what did you study?
If not, what did you do instead?

_____

_____

_____

_____

_____

_____

_____

_____

_____

> "A child's first teacher **IS ITS MOTHER.**"

PENG LIYUAN

PART II

PASSIONS & PURSUITS

Your passions make you uniquely you.
Who are you, and what do you believe to be true?

In this section, you have the opportunity to express your passions, pursuits, and personal beliefs. Consider your likes, dislikes, and interests as you respond to each question.

In the first part, you'll answer simple questions about a few of your favorite things. The remaining sections should prompt you to journal about the characteristics that make you unique and the values you hold dear.

Take the time to think about how your career decisions have influenced your life. You'll also be able to reflect on the nostalgic places and things that still matter to you today.

A FEW FAVORITES

What is a favorite food that you order out at a restaurant?
Is there anything special about the way it's prepared?

_____

_____

_____

_____

_____

_____

_____

_____

_____

_____

What is your favorite season? Describe why you prefer that time of year.

_____

_____

_____

_____

_____

_____

_____

_____

_____

_____

What is your favorite day of the week? Describe your
ideal day.

Where is a favorite place you've visited? What place have you not visited yet that you believe would be a favorite if you could just get there?

_____

_____

_____

_____

_____

_____

_____

_____

What is your favorite way to spend time outdoors?

In the end,
I am the only one
WHO
CAN GIVE MY
CHILDREN
a happy mother
who loves life.

JANENE WOLSEY BAADSGAARD

CAREER

What was the first job you had where you earned a paycheck?
How old were you?

_____

_____

_____

_____

_____

_____

_____

_____

_____

What was the best job you ever had? Why did you enjoy it?

What has helped you succeed most at work?

What's a career you find admirable but feel you could never do?

_____

_____

_____

_____

_____

_____

_____

_____

_____

_____

What is a job you would love to do if given the opportunity?

" MOST MOTHERS ARE instinctive philosophers. **"**

HARRIET BEECHER STOWE

BELIEFS

Did you grow up with a specific faith background? How does that align with your spiritual beliefs now?

_____

_____

_____

_____

_____

_____

_____

_____

_____

_____

_____

If you had to pick three core values to live by,
what would they be?

_____

_____

_____

_____

_____

_____

_____

_____

_____

_____

What wisdom has an older family member passed on to you that has helped shape your life?

_____

_____

_____

_____

_____

_____

_____

_____

_____

▼

What are three things you hope to **be remembered for**?

What is a good investment you've made with your
money or time?

_____

_____

_____

_____

_____

_____

_____

_____

_____

_____

**BEING
A MOTHER**
is learning about strengths
you didn't know
YOU HAD.

LINDA WOOTEN

NOSTALGIC PLACES & THINGS

Where was your favorite place to visit as a child? What is your fondest memory of your time there?

_____

_____

_____

_____

_____

_____

_____

_____

_____

_____

What is a food you enjoyed as a child that you still love today?

_____

_____

_____

_____

_____

_____

_____

_____

_____

What childhood activity did you love that kids don't seem to enjoy today?

_____

_____

_____

_____

_____

_____

_____

_____

What has been the most impactful decade of your life?
What year and specific event was the most significant?

_____

_____

_____

_____

_____

_____

_____

_____

_____

_____

What are simple things you enjoy today that make you nostalgic for the past? (Examples might be a sweet treat, television show, hobby, or pastime.)

_____

_____

_____

_____

_____

_____

_____

_____

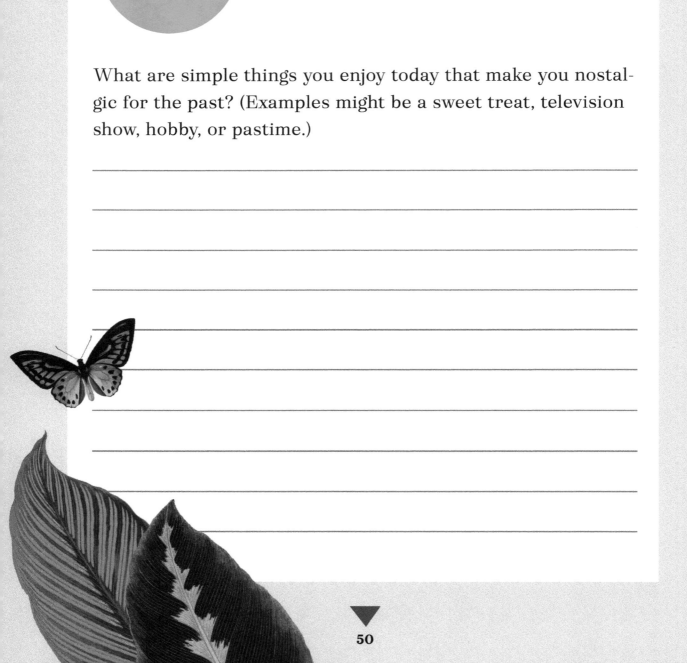

Sometimes the strength of
MOTHERHOOD
is greater than
NATURAL
LAWS.

BARBARA KINGSOLVER

PART III

LOVE & FRIENDSHIP

The quality of our relationships determines the quality of our lives. In part, we are shaped by the people we choose to spend the most time with. The people we invited to share in our lives have a meaningful role in our development into who we are today.

Our intimate relationships help us gain (or even lose) self-confidence, trust, and/or a sense of belonging.

This section invites you to think back to your first relational experiences and prompts you to explore the more intimate moments and memories shared between friends and romantic partners.

FIRSTS

Who was your first best friend? Where did you meet?

_____

_____

_____

_____

_____

_____

_____

_____

_____

_____

Who was your first crush? Which of their qualities attracted you to them?

What was your most memorable first date?

When did you first know you were in love? What experience made you realize this person was different than others?

_____

_____

_____

_____

_____

_____

_____

_____

_____

_____

Who was the first person to break your heart? Or were you the heartbreaker?

_____

_____

_____

_____

_____

_____

_____

_____

_____

_____

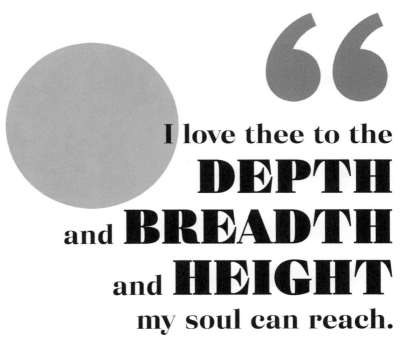

"I love thee to the **DEPTH** and **BREADTH** and **HEIGHT** my soul can reach."

ELIZABETH BARRETT BROWNING

FRIENDS

Who is your oldest friend and how many years have you remained friends? In what ways have you maintained this friendship?

_____

_____

_____

_____

_____

_____

_____

_____

_____

_____

Describe a time when friendship disappointed you or brought pain to your life. Was there a resolution?

_____

_____

_____

_____

_____

_____

_____

_____

_____

_____

What qualities do you value the most in a friend? Who is someone that embodies these traits?

_____

_____

_____

_____

_____

_____

_____

_____

_____

Describe a monumental moment you shared with a friend.

_____

_____

_____

_____

_____

_____

_____

_____

_____

_____

Describe a situation in which you showed up for a friend who was in need.

_____

_____

_____

_____

_____

_____

_____

_____

_____

_____

_____

"

There is a natural **EBB** and **FLOW** to friendships. The special ones **SURVIVE.**

"

COLETTE MCBETH

ROMANCE

Did your family have any rules for dating, and if so, what were
they? How old were you when you went on your first date?

_____

_____

_____

_____

_____

_____

_____

_____

_____

_____

_____

Describe a difficult decision that you had to make in a romantic relationship.

_____

_____

_____

_____

_____

_____

_____

_____

_____

_____

▼

What is a lesson you have learned about love that can be attributed to the relationships you have had through-out your life?

_____

_____

_____

_____

_____

_____

_____

_____

_____

What is the key to a healthy romantic relationship?

_____

_____

_____

_____

_____

_____

_____

_____

_____

_____

▼

What qualities are most valuable when looking for a
life partner?

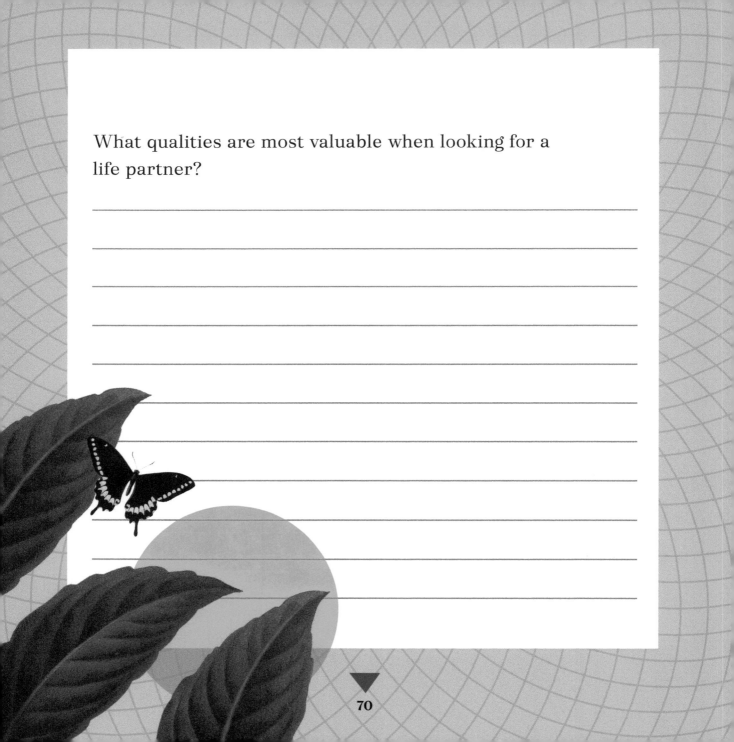

The best thing to hold onto in life is **EACH OTHER.**

AUDREY HEPBURN

SECRETS

What do you remember hiding from (or not sharing with) your family as a young adult?

_____

_____

_____

_____

_____

_____

_____

_____

_____

_____

Name a person you trust with your innermost secrets.
Why are you most comfortable sharing with them?

_____

_____

_____

_____

_____

_____

_____

_____

_____

Did you ever tell someone a secret you later wished you hadn't? Why did you regret telling them?

_____

_____

_____

_____

_____

_____

_____

_____

_____

Describe an experience from your adulthood that has shaped you into who you are today.

_____

_____

_____

_____

_____

_____

_____

_____

_____

_____

Is it easy or difficult for you to keep a secret when you think sharing it could help someone?
Why do you believe this to be true?

_____

_____

_____

_____

_____

_____

_____

_____

▼

Seldom, **VERY SELDOM,** does complete truth belong to any human **DISCLOSURE;** seldom can it happen that something is not a little disguised, or a little **MISTAKEN.**

JANE AUSTEN

PART IV

MATERNALLY YOURS

There's no stronger bond than the one between a mother and their child, yet we often don't have the opportunity to learn about a mother's heart. This section will paint a picture of your mother-hood journey and explore how this role has changed you.

These questions will prompt you to recall your child's early experiences. Some they may have been too young to remember. It is also a space to tell stories that can only be shared through your unique motherly perspective.

Take this time to reflect on the ways, whether expected or unexpected, that mother-hood has changed your expectations and priorities.

ALL ABOUT US

What are the most important things you have done to be able to enjoy raising your child or children?

_____

_____

_____

_____

_____

_____

_____

_____

_____

_____

Name and describe the toughest stage of motherhood for you. Was it when your child was a newborn, a toddler, a school-child, a teenager, or an adult?

_____

_____

_____

_____

_____

_____

_____

_____

_____

What parenting decision did you make where you felt unsupported in what you were doing?

_____

_____

_____

_____

_____

_____

_____

_____

_____

_____

Describe a moment in motherhood you will always remember.

_____

_____

_____

_____

_____

_____

_____

_____

_____

_____

Have you ever experienced "mom guilt"?

What happened to make you feel this way?

What makes you feel most confident as a mother?

_____

_____

_____

_____

_____

_____

_____

_____

_____

My mother shed her

PROTECTIVE LOVE DOWN AROUND ME

and without knowing
why people sensed that

I HAD VALUE.

MAYA ANGELOU

BECOMING A MOM

How or when did you find out you were going to be a mom?
What was your reaction?

_____

_____

_____

_____

_____

_____

_____

_____

_____

_____

Did you always want to have children? Why or why not?

_____

_____

_____

_____

_____

_____

_____

_____

_____

_____

What were your worries or fears about motherhood prior to having a child?

_____

_____

_____

_____

_____

_____

_____

_____

_____

_____

_____

Whose advice for raising children did you seek?
Why did you choose to listen to them?

_____

_____

_____

_____

_____

_____

_____

_____

_____

_____

How has motherhood changed you?

"MOTHER IS A VERB. It's something you do. Not just who **YOU ARE."**

DOROTHY CANFIELD FISHER

MILESTONES

What milestone did your child or children reach that was bittersweet for you?

_____

_____

_____

_____

_____

_____

_____

_____

_____

_____

What milestone of child rearing were you excited to finally reach?

_____

_____

_____

_____

_____

_____

_____

_____

_____

What milestone were you concerned your child or one of your children might never reach? At the time, what worries did you have?

Describe a milestone in your motherhood journey that filled you with strong emotion.

_____

_____

_____

_____

_____

_____

_____

_____

_____

_____

What milestone in your child's or children's life did you enjoy celebrating?

_____

_____

_____

_____

_____

_____

_____

_____

_____

_____

"Parenting is by far my **BOLDEST** and most daring **ADVENTURE.**"

BRENÉ BROWN

SHARED TRAITS

Does your child or children have any physical traits or learned behaviors that are similar to other family members?

_____

_____

_____

_____

_____

_____

_____

_____

_____

_____

What is a trait your child or children have that you wish
you possessed? Why?

_____

_____

_____

_____

_____

_____

_____

_____

_____

_____

What personality traits do you share with your child or children? In what ways are you complete opposites?

_____

_____

_____

_____

_____

_____

_____

_____

_____

_____

Name an activity you and your child or children both enjoy.

_____

_____

_____

_____

_____

_____

_____

_____

_____

_____

▼

Are there any family traits or behaviors – physical or
learned – that you hoped would not be passed down to your
child or children. Why?

_____

_____

_____

_____

_____

_____

_____

_____

_____

A mother's love for
HER CHILD
is like nothing else in
THE WORLD.

AGATHA CHRISTIE

PART V

LIFE LESSONS

Your hindsight can be another's greatest insight if you take the time to share what you've learned throughout your life and motherhood journey.

Passing on the lessons you've gained through your life experiences is an invaluable gift to future generations. Here is where you will share your view on how the world has changed in your lifetime and chronicle pivotal moments that developed your character and influenced your life.

In this section, you will reflect on your past, contemplate your future, and share the choices that have molded you into the individual and mother you are today.

THEN VS. NOW

Name a way that motherhood has been easier, or more difficult, for you than it possibly was for earlier generations of mothers.

_____

_____

_____

_____

_____

_____

_____

_____

_____

In what ways have you raised your child or children differently than how you were raised?

_____

_____

_____

_____

_____

_____

_____

_____

_____

_____

What past values do you feel are not being upheld
in today's society?

In what ways has the world changed over your lifetime?

_____

_____

_____

_____

_____

_____

_____

_____

_____

_____

How have the advancements of technology changed your life
for the better and the worse?

_____

_____

_____

_____

_____

_____

_____

_____

_____

_____

"NOTHING is ever really LOST TO US as long as we REMEMBER IT."

L.M. MONTGOMERY

— GENERATIONAL WISDOM —

Name a valuable lesson from your childhood and describe
how it has helped you as an adult.

_____

_____

_____

_____

_____

_____

_____

_____

_____

Recall a saying from a family member you find yourself repeating.

_____

_____

_____

_____

_____

_____

_____

_____

_____

_____

What is something you took for granted in the past that is
special to you now?

_____

_____

_____

_____

_____

_____

_____

_____

_____

_____

What are values your family shares and hopes that future generations will continue to pass on?

_____

_____

_____

_____

_____

_____

_____

_____

_____

_____

What is the most meaningful advice an elder has bestowed on you that has changed your life? In what way?

_____

_____

_____

_____

_____

_____

_____

_____

_____

The art of
MOTHERING
is to teach the art of
LIVING TO
CHILDREN.

ELAINE HEFFNER

OUR LEGACY

Who did you look up to as a child? Do you still admire them today?

_____

_____

_____

_____

_____

_____

_____

_____

_____

_____

What are the most important things you want future generations to know about you and what you stand for?

_____

_____

_____

_____

_____

_____

_____

_____

_____

_____

▼

Which material item would you grab if you had to
evacuate your home in the event of an emergency?
Why is it important to you?

What is something you collect that is meaningful to you?
Why did you start that collection?

_____

_____

_____

_____

_____

_____

_____

_____

_____

_____

What are you doing today to build the legacy you want to leave behind?

_____

_____

_____

_____

_____

_____

_____

_____

_____

How we **SPEND OUR DAYS IS,** of course, how we spend **OUR LIVES.**

ANNIE DILLARD

— CHOICES & DECISIONS —

What is a choice you remember making in opposition to what your parents thought you should do?

_____

_____

_____

_____

_____

_____

_____

_____

_____

_____

What is a tough decision that you felt confident to make?

_____

_____

_____

_____

_____

_____

_____

_____

_____

_____

Did you ever physically relocate in your life? Was this by choice? What did you learn through your experiences?

_____

_____

_____

_____

_____

_____

_____

_____

_____

Name a decision you have come to regret. Share your
philosophy on mistakes and/or regrets.

_____

_____

_____

_____

_____

_____

_____

_____

_____

_____

What is a brave decision you made where you learned a lot about yourself? How has this decision impacted your life?

_____

_____

_____

_____

_____

_____

_____

_____

_____

"

I BELIEVE that we are solely responsible for our **CHOICES,** and we have to accept the consequences of **EVERY DEED,** word, and **THOUGHT** throughout our lifetime.

ELISABETH KÜBLER-ROSS

"

REFERENCES

Angelou, Maya. *Mom & Me & Mom.* Random House, 2013.

Austen, Jane. *Emma.* 1815.

Baadsgaard, Janene Wolsey. *Grin & Share It: Raising a Family with a Sense of Humor.* Shadow Mountain, 1999.

Brown, Brené. *Daring Greatly.* Gotham Books, 2012.

Browning, Elizabeth Barrett. *Sonnets from the Portuguese,.* 1850.

Christie, Agatha. *The Hound of Death.* HarperCollins, 2008.

Dillard, Annie. *The Writing Life.* Harper Perennial, 1998.

Donovan, Cheryl Lacey. *The Ministry of Motherhood.* Peace in the Storm Publishing, 2009.

Heffner, Elaine. *Oprah Magazine,* May 2003.

Hepburn, Audrey. "13 of Audrey Hepburn's Most Inspiring Quotes." *Time.* May 4, 2016. Accessed August 30, 2020. www.time.com/4316700 /audrey-hepburn-inspiring-quotes/.

Howard, Jane. *Families.* Simon and Schuster, 1978.

Kingsolver, Barbara. *Homeland and Other Stories.* Harper Perennial, 1989.

Kübler-Ross, Elisabeth. EKR Foundation. Accessed August 16, 2020. www.ekr
foundation.org/elisabeth-kubler-ross/quotes/.

Liyuan, Peng. "Peng Liyuan Named UNESCO Special Envoy for the Advancement
of Girls' and Women's Education." Unesco. Accessed August 20, 2020.
https://en.unesco.org/news/peng-liyuan-named-unesco-special-envoy-advancement
-girls%0e2%080%099-and-women%0e2%080%099s-education.

McBeth, Colette. "Female Friendship Can Be Complex." *Telegraph.* July 29, 2013.
Accessed September 2, 2020. www.telegraph.co.uk/women/womens-life/10202594
/Female-friendship-can-be-complex.html.

Montgomery, L. M. *The Story Girl.* Quiet Vision Publishing, 2000.

Schaeffer, Edith. *What Is a Family?* Baker Books, 1975.

Stone, Elizabeth. "The Backstory of Steve Jobs' Quote About Parenthood." Gigaom.
October 11, 2011. Accessed August 21, 2020. https://gigaom.com/2011/10/11/419-the-long
-backstory-of-steve-jobs-quote-about-parenthood.

Stowe, Harriet Beecher. *The Minister's Wooing.* Sampson Low, Son, & Co., 1859.

Wooten, Linda. *Mother's Thoughts.* Winston-Derek Publishing, 1990.

ABOUT THE AUTHOR

AMY CARNEY is the author of *Parent on Purpose: A Courageous Approach to Raising Children in a Complicated World.* She is a public speaker, content creator, and product maker helping parents raise their children with more joy and purpose. She lives with her husband and five children in Paradise Valley, Arizona. You can learn more about her work at **AmyCarney.com.**

CPSIA information can be obtained
at www.ICGtesting.com
Printed in the USA
LVHW071738250821
695824LV00007B/7

9 781638 788546